Quarantinis by the Daves

100+ COCKTAIL RECIPES TO GET YOU THROUGH A LOCKDOWN

Dave Mastren

Dave Dunbar

Text and photographs by Dave Dunbar used with permission

Published by The Daves

ISBN: 979-8-9992110-0-2

Cover design by Lisa Brink (www.TheBrinkCreative.com)

Printed in the United States of America

INTRODUCTION

The idea for this book came about during a nationwide Covid-19 lockdown in the early spring of 2020. From the middle of March until the beginning of summer, much of America was under quarantine due to government issued stay-at-home orders. Two friends and former bartenders, Dave Mastren (California) and Dave Dunbar (Hawaii), along with our wives, Donna Mastren and Dawn Dunbar, decided to start a "dueling cocktails" challenge on a social media website as a way of staying touch and to alleviate the feeling of isolation by being stuck at home during the lockdown. We staged and photographed each cocktail and called our nightly offering, "The Quarantini".

This went on for about 8 weeks until we started to have more freedom and mobility and eventually the lockdown ended, as did the cocktail duel. We gathered up all the photos and dialogue from the social media website and made a photo book out of it through the photo department of a local warehouse club. The demand for the photo book was immediate and over-whelming among friends and family. Requests for the photo book continued, but it soon became increasingly expensive and eventually cost prohibitive after the warehouse company closed their photo business and sold it off to a high priced competitor. It was then that we made the decision to make it into a regular book of its own. We added some history to each cocktail to enhance the reading experience and gave a definition of each liqueur and garnish used as well as some homemade recipes, but we're sure you'll love the cocktails themselves.

The recipes in this book are a combination of our experiences as bartenders as well as recipes we took from a few of our favorite cocktail books. The photographs were staged in our homes in California and Hawaii and taken with our cell phones.

Enjoy, and stay safe.

The Daves

Dave Mastren and Dave Dunbar

LIQUEURS, GARNISHES AND HOME RECIPES USED IN THIS GUIDE

Absinthe - Absinthe is an herb-infused alcohol derived from fennel, anise, and the leaves and flowers of a small shrub called wormwood (otherwise known as Artemisia absinthium). It is very high in alcohol content, so use sparingly

Amaretto - Amaretto is an Italian liqueur with a sweet, nutty, and slightly honeyed taste and a pronounced almond flavor. It's made from apricot kernels, which give it a bitter almond taste, and brown sugar, which tones down the bitterness

Bailey's Irish Cream - Made with Irish cream, spirits, and Irish whiskey, and has aromas of coffee, hazelnut, and chocolate, with flavors of white chocolate, vanilla, and lightly toasted nuts, balanced by a smooth whiskey note

Benedictine - Benedictine is an herbal liqueur made in France. It is flavored with 27 herbs, berries, flowers, roots, and spices, including saffron, cinnamon, fir cones, juniper, honey, lemon balm, and angelica root. It has the flavor of sweet honey accented with holiday spices and stone fruits

Bitters - Bitters are a neutral alcohol infused with spices, herbs, fruits, roots, and other ingredients. Angostura bitters have strong baking-spice notes like allspice and cinnamon and a bitter finish. Peychauds bitters present an anise-forward, licorice-like flavor profile. Orange or grapefruit bitters offer a refreshing, citrusy twist

Campari - An Italian liqueur that's considered an amaro variety of apéritif. Its flavor is rife with intense orange peel, rhubarb, and bark

Candied Orange - Requires just 2-ingredients to make. 1 cup water in a sauce pan. Bring to a boil, add 1 cup sugar and stir until dissolved. Reduce heat to medium and add 1 orange sliced into about 6 slices. Let the orange slices cook at a gentle simmer for about 45 - 60 minutes. Use tongs to turn them over in the syrup every now and then. Use tongs to remove the slices from the sugar syrup and lay them out on a wire rack. Leave the orange slices on the wire rack to dry, uncovered, at room temperature for 24 - 48 hours

Chambord - Pronounced "sham boar" - A fruity, brandy-based liqueur made in the Loire Valley of France from black raspberries, red raspberries, blackberries and black currants. It also has notes of vanilla, citrus, and honey

Chilled glass - To chill a glass you can place it gently in the ice cubes, but a safer way would be by placing a few ice cubes in the glass, add a small bit of water and swirl it around

Coconut cream - Coconut cream has a rich texture and nostalgic sweetness. Coconut cream is made from coconut meat and water, and has a higher fat content and thicker consistency than coconut milk

Cognac - Cognac is a category of brandy named for the Cognac region in France where it is produced

Cointreau - A type of triple sec but a higher quality version with a significantly higher alcohol content (40 percent ABV). It is made from sweet and bitter orange peels, sugar beet alcohol, and water

Crème de cacao - Crème de cacao is a chocolate-flavored liqueur. White crème de cacao is clear in color and has flavors of milk chocolate. Dark crème de cacao is deep brown in color and is rich, bitter, and more cocoa flavored

Crème de cassis - Crème de cassis is a sweet, dark red liqueur made from black currants that are crushed and soaked in alcohol, with sugar subsequently added

Crème de menthe - Is a sweet mint liqueur derived from a distillate of mint leaves and is available to buy as bottles of either green or white (clear). Sweeter than a Peppermint Schnapps, but made much the same way

Curaçao - is an orange liqueur flavored with the dried peel of a bitter orange fruit gown on the Caribbean island of Curaçao. It can be sold in numerous forms, though the most common are the orange-hued dry Curaçao and blue Curaçao, which is dyed bright blue. It can be used as a substitute for triple sec in some cocktails

Galliano - Galliano is an Italian liqueur made from neutral alcohol that's steeped with herbs and spices. Some of the botanicals used include: juniper berries, caraway seed cloves, cardamom, sandalwood, star anise, cinnamon, sage, thyme, mint, and lavender. It has a sweet vanilla-anise flavor and subtle citrus and herbal undertones

Grand Marnier - (pronounced Grand Marn-Yay)
A French orange liqueur and cognac blend with a sweet but balanced taste with notes of candied orange, toffee, caramel, hazelnut, marmalade, fresh orange zest, and cognac

Grenadine - Usually store bought, but grenadine is made with a base of pomegranate juice, which is how it got its name — the French word for pomegranate is grenade. 1 cup white sugar, 1/2 cup pomegranate juice: Pour sugar and pomegranate juice into a sauce pan and warm over low heat until the sugar dissolves. (a squeeze of lemon is optional, but good). Cool, pour into a bottle or jar, and store sealed in the refrigerator

Kahlúa - Kahlúa is probably the most popular coffee liqueur. Made from rum, 100% Arabica coffee beans, and sugar. Other coffee liqueur substitutes are Tia Maria, Frangelico, Jameson cold brew and many others

Li hing mui powder - A sweet, sour, and savory spice that's a staple in Hawaiian cuisine. It typically contains the following ingredients: Licorice, red food coloring, salt, sugar, other sweeteners

Limoncello - Limoncello is a sweet and fresh Italian lemon liqueur that's typically produced in southern Italy. It's made by steeping lemon zest in a neutral, highly concentrated alcohol, such as grain-based or grape-based rectified spirit, for several weeks to release the oils. The alcohol is then strained and sweetened with simple sugar syrup

Liqueur de violette - Made from a maceration of violets

steeped in brandy with added sugars. Gin and lemon are natural partners for Crème de violette, with the floral components of the liqueur playing nicely with the herbal flavors and citrus

Midori - A melon liqueur that is a sweet, bright green liqueur made with neutral grain spirit, brandy, and sugar. The sweet flavor comes from two types of Japanese melons. It has a smooth finish and aromas of melon

Pellegrino - San Pellegrino is a brand of sparkling natural mineral water that comes from a natural spring in the Italian Alps. Made in different flavors

Prosecco - Prosecco is a sparkling wine mostly made in the Veneto region, Italy

Sambuca - This clear Italian liqueur is flavored with the essential oils from star anise or green anise, giving it the unmistakable character of licorice

Schnapps - Schnapps is a strong, clear, alcoholic beverage that can be flavored with fruit, herbs, spices, cream, or nuts. "Schnapps" comes from the German word schnaps, which means "to swallow" or "a shot"

Simple Syrup - 1 cup white sugar, 1 cup water: Combine in a saucepan over medium heat. Bring to a boil until the sugar has dissolved. Allow to cool. Store in a clean jar and seal with a tight lid. Will stay refrigerated for up to one month

Sweet and Sour - Typically store bought, but you can make your own! In a saucepan simmer 2 cups of water and 1 cup of granulated sugar over medium heat until it is dissolved. Pour into a jar and let it come to room temperature. Add 1/2 cup of lemon juice and 1/2 cup lime juice. Store it in a sealed container for a week or for up to a month in the freezer. Pro tip: microwave your lemons and limes for about 10 seconds then roll on the counter for extra juice

Triple Sec - A sweet, clear, orange-flavored liqueur. The name comes from the French phrase triple sec, which means "triple distilled". It is typically made by steeping dried orange peels in a neutral spirit, such as sugar beet, and then redistilling the mixture

Tuaca - A sweet, golden brown liqueur that's a blend of Italian brandy, citrus, vanilla, and other spices. It has a complex flavor that can range from hints of butterscotch and cola to notes of caramel and roasted coconut

Turbinado Sugar - A minimally processed form of cane sugar that retains some of its natural molasses, resulting in a golden-brown color and a slightly richer, caramel-like flavor compared to white sugar. For Turbinado simple syrup just replace white sugar with Turbinado sugar

Velvet Falernum - a low-proof liqueur with Caribbean flavors of lime, almond, vanilla, ginger, and cloves

Vermouth -an aromatized, fortified wine, flavored with various botanicals (roots, barks, flowers, seeds, herbs, and spices). Typically sweet (red) or dry (white)

Every bar needs a wide variety of glassware and it doesn't need to be fancy or expensive!

Essential Bar tools

Jigger - A 2 ended jigger is 1 oz on the small end and 2 oz on the large end. Each end has additional measuring lines for 1/2 or 3/4 oz

Paring knife - For cutting garnish. Hint: Keep it sharp!

Citrus peelers - To make twists or long fancy garnishes that hang off the glass

Cutting board - For cutting citrus for drinks or trimming garnishes like lemon or orange peels

Mixing can with strainer and long bar spoon - The spoon is used for stirring and the strainer keeps any muddled remnants out of your cocktails

Pint glass - Can be used over the shaker for extra vigorous shaking. Also good when you need a cold beer

Cocktail shaker - Don't skimp, get a good one

Stir sticks, straws, garnish picks - All necessary for a wide variety of cocktails

Pour spouts - Vital for a smooth flow and measure of alcohol and mixes

Juicer - Good for squeezing citrus as needed

Muddler - For muddling fruits or herbs or crushing berries

Bartenders wine opener - For obvious reasons - Don't skimp on this tool or you'll be pulling shredded cork out of your wine bottle

These tools will make your bartending experience easier and look more professional

The Cocktails

Beauty Spot

Fill a cocktail shaker with ice

1 oz gin

1/2 oz sweet vermouth

1/2 oz dry vermouth

1 oz orange juice

Shake until well chilled

Chill martini glass - pour in a dash of grenadine

Fill the glass with the contents of shaker

Are you ready for a LOCKDOWN !!! This cocktail dates as far back as
1914 and can be found in Jacques Straub's cocktail book "Drinks"

BERRY BRAMBLE

Fill a cocktail shaker with ice

In a small pan, cook 1 1/2 oz simple syrup along with 1/4 cup each
of blueberries, blackberries, raspberries, and a dash of cinnamon
and a dash of ground cloves

Add this mixture to the shaker then add

2 oz gin

1/2 oz lemon juice

Shake until chilled, strain into glass filled with ice

Top off with soda or Prosecco

The original is simply called The Bramble and the only berry used is the
blackberry. Being pie makers by trade, we embellished this recipe to
add raspberries and blueberries along with the cinnamon and cloves.
And everything goes with Prosecco, right?

¡VENEZUELA LIBRE!

Fill a cocktail shaker with ice

1 1/2 oz rum

1/2 oz fresh lime juice,

1/2 oz gin

2 dashes Angostura bitters

Shake and pour over ice

Fill with RC cola!

This is a Venezuelan variation of the Cuba Libre which is believed to
have originated in Havana, Cuba around 1900

BLUE CARNATION
Fill a cocktail shaker with ice
1 oz white crème de cacao
1 oz blue Curaçao
1 oz. light cream
Shake all ingredients until well chilled
Strain into chilled cocktail glass

This cocktail is a relatively new creation becoming popular with the
70's trend of blue-colored drinks. Light and creamy

BLACK DIAMOND SWIZZLE
Fill a hurricane glass with ice.
1 1/2 oz. dark rum
1/2 oz Campari
3/4 oz fresh lime juice
1/2 oz simple syrup
Drizzle Meyer's rum on top
Garnish with fresh strawberry

This is a recent creation that is a variant of the classic "Swizzle" cocktail believed to have originated in the Caribbean around 1932

Blue Hawaiian
In a blender add
1 scoop of ice
1 oz blue Curaçao
1 oz light rum
1 oz coconut cream
2 oz pineapple juice
Blend and pour into a hurricane glass
Garnish with a cherry and a pineapple slice

One sip and you're on Island time. Created in 1957 by the head
bartender of the Hilton Hawaiian Village in Waikiki, Hawaii

BOCCE BALL
Fill a glass with ice
1 1/2 oz Amaretto
1 oz orange juice
Fill with club soda

This one will beat the "Rona" blues. The origin of this cocktail is hazy, but is likely a 1970s creation possibly from New York, where Italian-American culture and the game of bocce were both thriving.

BLUE LAGOON
1oz blue Curaçao
1oz vodka
Pour over ice
Fill with lemonade
Garnish with lemon twist

This cocktail is believed to have originated from Harry's New York Bar
in Paris in the 1960s

BONNY DOON

Fill a cocktail shaker with ice
2 oz blended scotch whisky
1/2 oz Benedictine
Shake em up and pour over ice in a bucket glass

CUBAN ALMOND

Fill a rocks glass with ice
1 1/2 oz Amaretto
Fill with soda

Cuban Almond / Bonny Doon - Neither of these has a specific origin
being more modern creations, but give them a try, you'll thank me later

VIRGIN COLADA
Fill a glass with ice
2 oz coconut juice
2 oz pineapple juice

DAWN'S HAVANA
Fill a cocktail shaker with ice
Jigger (1 1/2 oz) of Malibu rum
1/2 oz lemon juice
1 oz pineapple juice
1 oz orange juice
Shake pour into a chilled martini glass

Virgin Colada / Dawn's Havana - The Virgin Colada's are for the kids.
Dawn's Havana was created just for this occasion. You saw it here first!

BOSTON COOLER
Fill a cocktail shaker with ice
1 1/2 oz rum
1 teaspoon powdered sugar
1/2 oz lemon juice,
Shake well and strain into a Collins glass filled with ice
Fill with club soda
Garnish with lemon twist

Originated in Massachusetts in the late 1800's - There are many revised
Mr. Boston bartenting guides. The first of which originated in 1935.
This one is coming to you from Mr. Boston: Official Bartender's Guide
by Anthony Giglio

Brandy Alexander

Fill a cocktail shaker with ice
1 1/2 oz brandy (or Cognac)
1 oz dark crème de cacao
1 oz cream
Shake until well chilled
Strain into a coupe glass
Garnish with grated nutmeg

This was originally a gin based cocktail, but the brandy version
emerged around the 1930s and quickly became more popular

BUSHWHACKER

Fill a bucket glass with ice
1/2 oz Amaretto
1/2 oz Kahlúa
1/2 oz, Bailey's
1/2 oz light rum
2 oz light cream

This one is a hit! - There are several interpretations of this one which
originated in the mid 1970s in Sapphire Village, St. Thomas

CAMPARI MINT SPRITZ
1 oz Campari
1 oz cranberry juice
3 oz Prosecco
Pour over ice and stir
Bruise a few mint leaves with your nubs and stir them in

Very good drink and an excellent way to use your Prosecco in a productive manner. - The drink originated from, where else, Italy in the late 1800s

CAFÉ AMORE
"COFFEE OF LOVE"
In a coffee cup add
1 oz Cognac (or brandy)
1 oz Amaretto
Add espresso (single or double) or black coffee
Top with frothed milk or whipped cream
Garnish with shaved almonds

AMORE! A more modern cocktail, but it's a good one - A French variation of the Irish Coffee, believed to have originated in Paris, France

WESTERN SOUR
Fill a cocktail shaker with ice
2 oz whiskey
1 oz fresh grapefruit juice
1/2 oz fresh lime
1/2 oz Velvet Falernum
1/4 oz Turbinado simple syrup
1 dash of grapefruit bitters
Garnish with a cherry

I think this is right! - This one emerged in the early 1960s during the
heyday of the tiki craze and the Kon-Tiki chain of restaurants - We
"borrowed" this recipe from our local chop house

Whiskey Smash

Muddle 4 or 5 mint leaves and 2 lemon wedges in a shaker

Pour in a 1 1/2 oz jigger of bourbon

3/4 oz simple syrup

Add a scoop of ice

Shake until well chilled

Strain a couple of times and pour over ice in a small bucket glass

Clap a mint leaf in your hands and use as garnish

This one's a winner! - A variation of the Mint Julep that first appeared
in a bartenders guide that dates clear back to 1887

CARIBBEAN CRUISE
Fill a cocktail shaker with ice
1 / 2 oz vodka
1 / 2 oz Malibu rum
1 / 2 oz Bacardi light rum
Shake it up
Add 1/4 oz, grenadine to a tall glass
Strain contents of shaker into glass
Fill with pineapple juice
Garnish with a cherry

There is no xact origin of this one but there are many variations. It is
certainly a refreshing tropical drink and is popular on the Islands

CAPE CODDER (OR CAPE CAHDDAH)
This is for our neighbors Sheila and Joe...
Fill a highball glass with ice
1 1/2 oz vodka
2 oz cranberry juice
Garnish with lime squeeze and top with fresh cranberries

A couple of these and you'll fahget whe ya pahked the kah! - This
cocktail originated in the 1940s as a marketing ploy by Ocean Spray.
Initially named Red Devil, it became the Cape Codder in the 1960s

CHAMBORD LEMONADE
Fill a cocktail shaker with ice
1 oz Chambord
1 oz vodka,
Juice of 1/2 lemon
2 oz simple syrup.
Shake and pour over ice in a Collins glass

Where's the Pig? - Chambord is a French raspberry liqueur that was
first introduced in 1982 in France. Adding the lemonade makes it a
great summer cocktail

CINNAMON MAPLE BOURBON SOUR
Fill a cocktail shaker with ice
2 oz bourbon
1 oz lemon juice
3 tablespoons maple syrup
1 teaspoon ground cinnamon
Shake well and pour into glass filled with ice

The girl who hates whiskey really likes this one! - It attracts the
neighbors too! This cocktail is a play on the Whiskey Sour which has its
origins in the late 1800s. Adding the cinnamon and maple really kicks it
up a notch

Rob Roy
Put a large ice cube in an old fashioned glass
3/4 oz sweet vermouth
1 3/4 oz scotch
Dash of Angostura bitters
Garnish with a cherry

Whiskey Daisy
Fill a cocktail shaker with crushed ice
2 oz whiskey
1 oz lemon juice
1/4 oz simple syrup
1/2 oz Grand Marnier
Shake until chilled then strain into a coupe glass
Fill with club soda

Rob Roy: Iis a Scottish version of the Manhattan and is believed to have been created in 1894 in New York. Whiskey Daisy: Has many variations and evolved from a whiskey sour over time

GIMLET
Fill a cocktail shaker with ice
1 tsp powdered sugar
1 oz lime juice
1 1/2 oz gin
Shake until well chilled
Pour in a martini glass
Garnish with lime wheel

COBBLER
Fill a glass with ice
1 1/2 oz gin
1 tsp powdered sugar
3 oz club soda
Garnish with a lime

Gimlet: Believed to have been created by a British Royal Navy doctor in the 19th century as an "anti-scurvy" medication. Cobbler: A variation of the cobbler family of cocktails. It also originated in the early 19th century

Cosmopolitan

Fill a cocktail shaker with ice
2 oz vodka (or gin)
1 oz cranberry juice
3/4 oz fresh lime juice
3/4 oz triple sec
Shake until well chilled
Strain into martini glass
Garnish with an orange twist

Cosmo! A fruity play on the Martini, believed to have originated either in the late 1970s in Miami, or in the late 1980s by a New York bartender and certainly popularized as Carrie Bradshaw's signature cocktail in Sex in the City

DAIQUIRI

Fill a cocktail shaker with ice
2 oz light rum
1/2 oz lime juice
1/2 oz simple syrup
Shake until well chilled
Strain into a coupe glass
Garnish with a lime

A Cuban classic that originated in 1898 near the town of, you guessed it..., Daiquiri

GOLDEN CADILLAC
Add 1 scoop ice into a blender
1 oz Galliano
1 oz white crème de cacao
2 oz half-and-half
Blend until smooth
Pour into glass
Add long straw

Don't forget your bartender! Created in 1952 by bartender Frank Cline
at Poor Red's in a tiny Sierra Nevada Foothill town near Placerville

DARK AND STORMY
Fill a glass with ice
1/2 oz fresh lime juice
2 oz dark rum (the original uses Goslings brand)
3 oz ginger beer
Garnish with a lime squeeze

Originated in Bermuda in the mid 1800s by the Royal Navy's officers'
club

WHISKEY SQUIRT
Fill a cocktail shaker with ice
1 3/4 oz whiskey
1 teaspoon powdered sugar
1/4 oz grenadine
Shake well and strain in a glass filled with ice
Fill with club soda
Garnish with a strawberry

Surf's up! - ok, how about bottoms up! - There are several variations of
this one. It's been around since the late 1940s

DAVE AND MIKE'S MIDORI ILLUSION
Fill a cocktail shaker with ice
2 oz Midori melon liqueur
1/2 oz mango vodka
1/2 oz triple sec
2 oz pineapple juice
1 oz lemon juice
Shake well until chilled
Fill a cocktail glass with ice
Strain into glass

Where's Mike? The origins of this cocktail are obscure, but it gained popularity in the 1980s particularly in Australia and the UK. This one was embellished a bit by Dave and Mike

ZIPPER
1 oz Chambord
1 oz vodka
Pour over ice in a Collins glass
Fill with 7-up
Garnish with mint leaves

Another one with obscure origins, but is most likely a product of the
1990's and early 2000's when vodka based drinks and flavored liqueurs
were dominating the nightclub and casual bar menus. it's taste is fun,
refreshing, and it's very easy to make

DOLCE VITA
(A SWEET LIFE)
In a cocktail shaker filled with ice
1 1/2 oz Amaretto
3/4 oz triple sec
1 oz orange juice
1 oz pineapple juice
Squeeze of lemon
Dash of cream
Shake well and strain into glass

A sweet life indeed! This cocktail also has several variations, but this is
the one we like

DUBLIN ICED COFFEE
In a tall glass add
2 oz strong cold-brewed coffee
2 oz stout (like Guinness)
1 1/2 oz Irish whiskey
3/4 oz simple syrup
Fill the glass with ice
Gently pour 1/2 oz heavy cream
Garnish with freshly grated cinnamon

ITALIAN SPRITZ
Fill a wine glass 1/2 full with ice
1 1/2 oz Aperol (sweeter) or Campari (drier)
3 oz Prosecco
3/4 oz soda
Garnish with an orange wheel

Dublin Iced Coffee: Is a twist on the classic Irish Coffee and served cold instead of hot. Italian Spritz: Originated in Veneto, Italy in the 1800s

FRENCH 75
Fill a cocktail shaker with ice
1 oz gin
1/2 oz lemon juice
1/2 oz simple syrup
Shake well until chilled then strain into champagne glass
Fill glass with champagne
Garnish with lemon twist

Cheers! This one originated at Harry's New York bar in Paris during
WW1 and named after the French 75mm field gun

Espresso Martini

Fill a cocktail shaker with ice

1 1/2 oz gin or vodka

3/4 oz coffee liqueur (I used Frangelico)

1 shot espresso

Shake until chilled then pour into a chilled martini glass

Add a layer of frothed cream if desired

Garnish with whole coffee beans

Here's mud in your eye! - Now a worldwide classic, but it's believed to have been created in London in the 1980s by a British bartender who made it for a young model who needed a pick-me-up while getting buzzed at the same time

FRENCH COLADA
Fill a cocktail shaker with ice
1 oz light rum
1/2 oz Cognac (or brandy)
1 oz cream
1/2 oz crème de cassis
1/2 oz coconut cream
1 oz pineapple juice
Shake em up!
Pour in coupe or martini glass

A play on the Pina Colada which originated in 1954. I guess adding the Cognac makes it French!

STRAWBERRY DAIQUIRI, (FROZEN)

Fill a blender with ice (or use crushed ice)
2 oz light rum
1 oz strawberry syrup
2 oz sweet and sour
A couple of fresh strawberries
Blend until slushy
Pour into a goblet wine glass
(Optional) Top with 1 oz Captain Morgan rum
Garnish with fresh strawberry and umbrella

A fruity play on a Daiquiri that couldn't be more refreshing while
you're lounging by poolside on a hot day

PINEAPPLE/MANGO MARGARITA, (FROZEN)
2 or 3 scoops of ice in a blender
1 3/4 oz tequila
3/4 oz triple sec
1/4 cup fresh mango chunks
1/4 cup fresh pineapple chunks
1 oz pineapple juice
1/2 oz fresh lime juice
1/4 oz simple syrup
Blend until slushy
Salt the rim of a wine goblet
Pour blended contents into glass
Garnish with lime wheel, pineapple, fresh mango

There are many stories about the origins of the
Margarita but the most popular belief is that it was
invented in the 1930s or 1940s in Mexico. This is a
refreshing twist on a classic

GANGSTER MARTINI
Fill a cocktail shaker with ice
1 oz Tuaca
1 oz Amaretto
1 oz vodka
1 1/2 oz pineapple juice
Shake until well chilled
Strain into a martini glass
Garnish with a red cherry

"Leave the gun, take the cannoli" - This one has an Italian twist on a
long established classic cocktail, the Martini. Capeesh!

Martini Up, dry, with two olives
In a cocktail shaker take 1/2 oz dry vermouth
Shake it with ice then strain it all out
Pour 2 oz gin over that ice and shake again
Garnish with 2 martini olives

Vodka Tonic
Fill glass with Ice
1 1/2 oz vodka
Fill with tonic water
Garnish with a lime squeeze

Happy 18th Anniversary - Martini: Maybe there's a better way to make
a dry Martini, but I haven't found it yet. Vodka Tonic: The vodka tonic
is a simple and refreshing variation of the gin and tonic which emerged
in the mid-19th century .

HOLE IN ONE
Fill a cocktail shaker with ice
1 1/2 oz scotch
3/4 oz sweet vermouth
1/2 tsp lemon juice
1 dash orange bitters
Shake until well chilled
Strain into a chilled rocks glass
Garnish with an orange twist

Scotch originated in ,where else, Scotland, as did golf.
Put them together and…..… "FORE"

56

Japanese Gin and Tonic
Fill a glass with ice
1 1/2 oz gin
2 oz tonic water
Add 1/2 oz Midori melon liqueur and stir
Garnish with lime or lemon wheel

乾 Kanpai — Cheers - The Gin and Tonic has been around since the
1840s. Adding the Midori is a relatively new twist on an old favorite

Gin Rosa
Fill a glass with ice
1 1/2 oz gin
1/2 oz dry vermouth
3 oz Pellegrino blood orange
Garnish with candied orange

This one is easy to take - Baby Mie likes them too! - From England in the mid-19th century. The original of this cocktail uses Angostura bitters but we substituted the Pellegrino blood orange as a refreshing twist

GIN FIZZ
Fill a cocktail shaker with ice
2 oz gin
1 tsp powdered sugar
Juice of 1/2 lemon
Shake and pour over ice
Fill with club soda

Even the dog wants one! The Gin Fizz has many variations and dates
back to at least the 19th century. This cocktail was often cited as a
hangover cure (good luck with that)

DEEP BLUE SEA MARTINI
Fill a cocktail shaker with ice
2 oz vodka
1/2 oz sweet and sour
1/2 oz pineapple juice
3/4 oz blue Curaçao.
Shake 'em up and strain into a martini glass
Garnish with a lemon twist

Caution, this one's dangerous! - The martini dates back to the 1860s
with this variation originating during a much more recent fad of blue
drinks from the 1970s and '80s

SHIRLEY TEMPLE
Fill glass with 7-up
Float 1/2 oz grenadine

GIN RICKEY
Fill a Collins glass with ice
1 1/2 oz gin
Juice from 1/2 lime
Fill with club soda
Gin Rickey is old school, and very refreshing
Garnish with a lime wedge

Photo shows one has a lighter color. Miss sweet tooth requested 7-up
instead of soda. The Shirley Temple originated in the 1930s when a
bartender made it for, guess who… The Gin Rickey originated in the
1880s in Washington D.C. and named after a Colonel, Joe Rickey

JOSE AND OJ
Pretty self-explanatory
2 oz Jose Cuervo tequila
2 oz orange juice

WHITE LADY
Fill a cocktail shaker with ice
1 3/4 oz gin
3/4 oz triple sec
1/2 oz fresh lemon juice
Shake well and strain into coupe glass
Garnish with an orange twist

Jose and OJ / White Lady - Cigar is optional 😎 - Jose
Cuervo has been around since 1758 and any citrus
drink is an easy addition. The White Lady dates back to
1929 from Harry's New York Bar in Paris

LAVA FLOW
In a blender add a handful of strawberries
1 1/2 oz light rum
1 1/2 oz Malibu rum
Blend to a purée
Add to a glass
Clean da blender!
Add 2 oz coconut cream
2 oz pineapple
Scoop of ice
Blend 'em again
Pour over strawberry puree

Make a blender of these and you're on vacation! - As
you might suspect, the Lava Flow originated in Hawaii
in the 1980s or '90s

KIR ROYALE

Chill a champagne flute or white wine glass
1/2 oz crème de cassis
Fill with champagne
Garnish with raspberries

Smile! - This cocktail originated in France in the 1940s and is named
after Canon Felix Kir, a Catholic priest and Mayor of Dijon during the
time the French resistance was active

Margarita Classica / Li hing Margarita
In a blender add a scoop of ice and
1 1/2 oz tequila
1/2 oz Cointreau
1 oz lime juice
1 1/2 oz sweet and sour mix
1/2 oz pureed mango
Blend and pour into a glass with Li hing mui powder on the rim
(on the right)
or regular coarse salt (on the left)
Garnish with a lime wedge

Margarita Classica / Li hing Margarita - Shirley Temples in the middle.
The Li hing Margarita is a Hawaiian creation that emerged from a
fusion of Chinese and Hawaiian culinary traditions

GRASSHOPPER
Fill a cocktail shaker with ice
1 oz green crème de menthe
1 oz white crème de cacao
1 oz light cream
Shake and pour on ice!
Garnish with fresh mint leaves

Even Grandma Jayne loved it! Happy Sunday from Oahu! - Originated in New Orleans in 1918 by restaurant owner Philbert Guichet, for a cocktail competition in New York where it took second place

LIBERTY COCKTAIL
Fill an old fashioned glass with ice
1 3/4 oz apple brandy
3/4 oz light rum
1/2 oz simple syrup
Garnish with a squeeze of lime

The origins are unclear, but this cocktail dates clear back to 1935 and is
a popular cocktail for 4th of July celebrations

LONE TREE COOLER
In a Collins glass add
2 oz gin
1/2 tsp powdered sugar
Stir in glass
Fill glass with ice
Add 1/2 oz dry vermouth
Fill with ginger ale or club soda
Garnish with orange and lemon twist

Another variation of the Martini that dates back to the early 1900s

LONELINESS
Fill a cocktail shaker with ice
1 1/2 oz vodka
1 dash Angostura bitters
3/4 oz lemon juice
1/2 oz simple syrup
1/8 teaspoon (a couple of drops) vanilla extract
1 egg white
Shake until well chilled
Strain into a cocktail glass filled with ice

"They're sharing a drink they call Loneliness cuz it's better than drinkin' alone" ♪♫♪♫ - There are several variations of this one and the origins are not certain, although Billy Joel could take credit for making it popular

MAIDEN'S BLUSH
Fill a cocktail shaker with ice
1 1/2 oz gin
3/4 oz triple sec
1/2 oz lemon juice
Splash of grenadine
Shake until well chilled
Strain into a martini glass
Garnish with a lemon twist

Yet another one with many versions, some that date as far back as 1896
- It is believed to have originated in Paris

MANGO SUNSET
Fill a cocktail glass with cubed ice
1 3/4 oz mango vodka
1 oz orange juice
1 oz cranberry juice
Garnish with a cherry

A creative use for the Mango vodka someone left in our liquor cabinet -
also called a Madras and originated in the 1940s. It is believed to have
been inspired by the beautiful sunsets on tropical beaches around the
world

MANHATTAN ON THE ROCKS
Fill a tumbler with ice
1/2 oz sweet vermouth
1 1/2 oz bourbon
1 dash Angostura bitters
Garnish with a cherry

WHISKEY SOUR
In a cocktail shaker add
2 oz whiskey
1 egg white
3/4 oz lemon juice
1/2 oz simple syrup
Shake for 30 seconds
Add ice and shake for another 30 seconds
Strain into a coupe glass
Garnish with a cherry and twist of lemon

Whiskey Sours / Manhattan in the middle. The Manhattan was created at the Manhattan Club in New York City in the mid 1870s. The Whiskey Sour is believed to have been created in the mid 1800s and appears in "The Bartender's Guide" in 1862 - Saddle Up!

Eagle's Dream
Fill a cocktail shaker with ice
1 1/2 oz gin
1/2 oz liqueur de violette
1/2 oz fresh lemon juice
1 egg white
1/2 oz simple syrup
Shake until well chilled then strain into an "up" glass
Garnish with a cherry or lemon twist

Goes good with pie! - First found in the "The Savoy Cocktail Book" in 1930

MANHATTAN UP

Fill a cocktail shaker with ice
3/4 oz sweet vermouth
1 1/2 oz bourbon
Shake until well chilled
Strain into a martini glass
Garnish with a cherry

Bada Bing! - Originated in New York City in the mid 1870s

Marble Queen
Fill a cocktail shaker with ice
1 1/2 oz tequila
1 oz coconut cream
1/2 oz fresh lime juice
Shake well and pour over ice into a small bucket with a
salted rim
Garnish with a lime squeeze

Buenos Tacos! - This one first appeared in 1951 in Ted Saucier's
"Bottoms Up" cocktail book and was "rediscovered" at the Zig Zag Cafe
in Seattle in the early 2000s

MARASCHINO CHERRY

Scoop of ice in a blender
1oz light rum
1/2 oz Amaretto
1/2 oz peach schnapps
1 oz cranberry juice
1 oz pineapple juice
A dash of grenadine
Blend, then top with whipped cream and a cherry

Make you strong, like Mie! - Another one with multiple variations, but the combination of these ingredients will at least make you happy, if not strong

Margarita (Joe-garita)
This is for our friend and neighbor Joe
Rim a glass with lime, dip in kosher salt
2 scoops of ice in a blender (or on the rocks)
1 3/4 oz tequila
3/4 oz triple sec
1/2 oz fresh lime juice
Garnish with a lime wheel

Joe-garita - The Margarita has been around since the 1930s-'40s and
Joe's version has been around since we moved in across the street from
him in the mid 1990s

WALLIS COCKTAIL
Fill a cocktail shaker with ice
1/2 oz Cointreau
1/2 oz peppermint schnapps
1 1/2 oz gin
1/4 oz lemon juice
Shake well pour over ice in a Collins glass
Fill with club soda
Garnish with lemon twist

This one has been linked to Wallis Simpson and Edward VIII, the Duke of Windsor, during their "scandalous" time together in the 1930s. It is a light and refreshing summer beverage

MOJITO

Muddle a couple if mint leaves in a shaker
2 oz light rum
3/4 oz fresh lime juice
1/2 oz simple syrup
Shake until well chilled
Fill a glass with ice and strain over the ice
Fill with club soda
Garnish with a lime wheel and a sprig of mint

I enjoyed this with a fine cigar - The Mojito is believed to have
originated in Havana, Cuba, in the 16th century with its earliest form
known as "El Draque", possibly named after Sir Francis Drake

Naked Pretzel
1 oz vodka
3/4 oz Midori melon liqueur
1/2 oz crème de cassis
2 oz pineapple juice
Pour over ice in an old fashioned glass

Can't say I care for the name, but this nostalgic recipe is from a Mr.
Boston cocktail guide. It's from an era of wild drinks and is actually a
refreshing tropical cocktail

NEGRONI
In a rocks glass filled with ice
3/4 oz sweet vermouth
1 1/4 oz gin
1 oz Aperol (or Campari if you like it real dry)
Garnish with orange wheel

The origin of the Negroni comes from Caffe Casoni in Florence, Italy in 1919. **Cool tip,** make this with bourbon (or rye) instead of gin and it's called a Boulevardier

MIDORI ILLUSION
Fill a glass with ice
2 oz Midori melon liqueur
1/2 oz pineapple vodka
1/2 oz triple sec
2 oz pineapple juice
Garnish with homemade candied oranges and (Marty Feldman)
cherries

This cocktail became popular in the 1980s with the introduction of
Midori liqueur in 1978.

OLD FASHIONED

In a cocktail glass
Muddle a sugar cube or add 1/2 oz simple syrup
Fill glass with ice
2 oz Kentucky bourbon or rye whiskey
3 dashes Angostura bitters
Garnish with an orange slice

This one will bring the band back together! As soon as we're allowed, of
course. This originated in the early 1800s and was named Old
Fashioned as a reliable drink and a reaction to the more complicated
cocktails of the time

Opal Cocktail
Fill a cocktail shaker with ice
1 oz gin
1/2 oz triple sec
1/4 oz OJ
1 tsp powdered sugar
Shake em up and pour in a chilled cocktail glass
Garnish with an orange twist

Another variation, but as a martini drinker I enjoyed this - A 1920's classic

MONTE CARLO IMPERIAL
Fill a cocktail shaker with ice
1/2 oz gin
1 /4 oz lemon juice
1/4 oz white crème de menthe
Shake until well chilled
Strain into a champagne glass
Fill glass with champagne

Bon appétit! - Adapted from the 1930 The Savoy Cocktail Book by
Harry Craddock, and also in Difford's Guide for Discerning Drinkers

THE PAN AMERICAN CLIPPER
Put a martini glass in the freezer to chill
Fill a cocktail shaker with ice
2 oz apple brandy
1/2 oz fresh lemon juice
1/2 oz fresh lime juice
3/4 oz grenadine
Shake until well chilled
Remove glass from freezer and coat lightly with Absinthe
(pour out any excess)
Strain contents of shaker into glass

This one just might kill the virus! - Originated in 1939 and named for a
pilot from Pan Am Airlines

PEACH MARGARITA
Add a scoop of ice in a blender then add
1 1/2 oz tequila
1/2 oz triple sec
1/2 oz fresh lime juice
1/2 oz peach brandy
1/2 fresh peach
2 oz sweet and sour
Blend and pour into a glass with a salted rim
Garnish with a squeeze of lime

The Margarita has been around since the mid-20th century and adding peaches makes it, well, just peachy

PINK LEMONADE

Fill a glass with ice
1 3/4 oz vodka
3/4 oz triple sec
1/2 oz lime juice
1 oz sweet and sour mix
1 oz cranberry
Garnish with a squeeze of lime

Not your kids' pink lemonade! This is another one with several recipe
variations, but this one makes a great summer drink

PIÑA COLADA
a cocktail shaker with ice
1 3/4 oz rum
1/2 oz coconut cream
3/4 oz pineapple juice
Shake until well chilled
Strain into a tumbler filled with ice
Garnish with a slice of pineapple

Always a favorite on a hot day! - Originated from Puerto Rico in the
1950s

Pink Paradise
Fill a glass with ice
1 1/2 oz Malibu rum
1 oz Amaretto
3 oz cranberry
1 1/2 oz pineapple juice

There are several variations and names for this delicious cocktail (Dave Matthew's, Italian Surfer), but whatever you call it, it's like a delicious fruit punch. Drink up!

RASPBERRY, LIMONCELLO AND PROSECCO COOLER

Put a glass and 3 or 4 raspberries in the freezer

Chill for 15 minutes

When ready, slap a fresh sprig of mint between your palms and put it in the glass

Add the raspberries then pour

1 oz limoncello

4 oz Prosecco

Cool and refreshing! Goes great with a shrimp cocktail - The original Prosecco cooler originated in the 1800s in Veneto, Italy. The raspberry and limoncello add a nice touch

Ramos Fizz

Fill a cocktail shaker with ice
2 oz dry gin
1 oz cream
Dash of flour water
1 oz simple syrup
1 small egg white
1/2 oz lime juice
1/2 oz lemon juice
Shake until well chilled
Strain into a Collins glass half-filled with ice
Fill with soda water
Garnish with orange

This one's old school! Shirley Temples on the left -
Originally called the New Orleans Fizz. Was invented in
1888 by Henry C. Ramos at his bar in New Orleans

93

ROMEO AND JULEP
In a cocktail glass muddle
1/2 tsp brown sugar
3 sprigs of mint
1/2 oz of peach schnapps
Fill glass with ice
Add 1 1/2 oz bourbon
Fill glass with 7-up
Garnish with mint leaves

A play on the Mint Julep which has its origins in the Middle East and
evolved in America with early settlers, particularly in Kentucky

Rhubarb Pie

Cook down 6 oz of rhubarb with 1/2 cup water and 1/4 cup
sugar in a pan until it turns to a juice/pulp
Strain mixture in a fine strainer, retain just the juice
Discard the pulp
In a cocktail shaker filled with ice add
2 oz gin or vodka
1 oz rhubarb juice
Shake until well chilled
Strain in a glass half filled with pebble sized ice
Fill with soda water
Garnish with slice of strawberry
Optional... rim the glass with granulated sugar mixed with
ground cinnamon

Likely emerged from the culinary traditions of rhubarb
use in both food and drinks (and pie!)

Rum Relaxer
Fill a cocktail shaker with ice
Jigger (1 1/2 oz) light rum
1/2 oz grenadine
1 oz pineapple juice
Shake it up and pour on ice
Fill glass with 7up!
Garnish with a pineapple slice or lemon wedge

Inspired by the Caribbean. A very refreshing summer drink

SAGE BROWN DERBY
Fill a cocktail shaker with ice
2 oz rye whiskey
1 oz fresh red or pink grapefruit juice
1/2 oz fresh lime juice
1/4 oz agave syrup
2 dashes grapefruit bitters
1 fresh sage leaf
Shake until frosty then strain into a glass
Slap a sage leaf between your palms to release the aromatics and
garnish on top

The Brown Derby cocktail was created in 1930 in
Hollywood. The Sage adds an earthy touch, making it a
great libation

STORK CLUB
Fill a cocktail shaker with ice
1 1/2 oz gin
1/2 oz triple sec
1/2 oz fresh lime juice
1 oz fresh orange juice
1 dash Angostura bitters
Shake well until chilled
Strain into a coupe or martini glass
Garnish with a slice of orange

Happy 21st Birthday, Teenie!!! - This one was invented
in 1946 by Stork Club bartender Eddie Whittmer

ITALIAN WINE AND SAMBUCA
Italian cold cuts - cheese, olives, salami, etc...
A bottle of tuscan red wine
A sip of Sambuca for dessert

È una cosa bellissima - "It's a beautiful thing" for you non Italians -
Italian wine dates back to the 8th century. The anise-flavored Sambuca
liqueur is believed to have originated near Rome in the mid-19th
century

SAZERAC

(This is for my father-in-law, Bob Chavez)
Place a rocks glass in the freezer to chill
Fill a cocktail shaker with ice
2 oz rye whiskey
1/2 oz simple syrup (or muddle 1 sugar cube)
4 dashes Peychaud bitters
1 dash Angostura bitters
Shake or stir until well chilled
Take rocks glass from the freezer and coat with Absinthe (pour
out any excess)
Pour the contents of shaker into the rocks glass
Add a twist of lemon peel for added flavor

Combine this with a Shrimp Louie, in a dimly lit corner booth with diamond tuck 'n' roll upholstery and some swing music, and you'll be living Bob's dream

SINGAPORE SLING

Fill a cocktail shaker with ice
1 1/2 oz gin
1/2 oz cherry brandy
1/4 oz Cointreau
1/4 oz Benedictine
2 oz pineapple juice
1/2 oz fresh lime juice
1 dash Angostura bitters
Shake until well chilled
Fill a Collins glass with ice
Strain into the glass
Top off with soda
Garnish with a cherry and an orange

Always a classic! - Believed to have been created at the Long Bar of the
Raffles Hotel in Singapore in 1915

SIDECAR

Coat the rim of a coupe glass with sugar
Fill a cocktail shaker with ice
1 1/2 oz Cognac
3/4 oz Cointreau
3/4 oz fresh lemon juice
Shake until chilled then strain into glass
Garnish with an orange twist

♫♫♫ Nice and easy does it every time ♫♫♪ - The origins for this one has multiple claims from London to Paris in the early 1920s

STILETTO MANHATTAN
Fill a cocktail shaker with ice
2 oz whiskey
1/2 oz Amaretto
3/4 oz dry vermouth
1 dash orange bitters
Shake until well chilled then strain into glass
Garnish with an orange twist and a cherry
Can be served up or on the rocks

Another one of the many variations of the traditional Manhattan,
which has been around since the late 1800s

STINGER
In a cocktail shaker filled with ice
2 oz cognac
1 oz white crème de menthe
Shake and strain into a tumbler filled with crushed ice, or up, in
a coupe glass

A good "after dinner" cocktail - The origins are believed to be from the late 1890's. It gained popularity in New York City and became known as a "society drink"

TROPICAL BREEZE
Fill a cocktail shaker with ice
1 1/2 oz pineapple vodka
2 oz cranberry juice
Shake or stir until well chilled
Pour in martini glass

Had to find a way to use a bottle of pineapple Vodka.
Tastes nothing like a cosmo; good though

STRAWBERRY DAWN
Add a scoop of ice to a blender
1 1/2 oz gin,
1 1/2 oz coconut cream
4 strawberries
Blend with ice and pour into a tall glass
Garnish with a strawberry

Mie Approves! - Difficult to pinpoint its origins as it is relatively
modern creation arising from trends and adaptations of existing
recipes, but trust us, this is a good one

Moscow Mule

Fill a cocktail shaker with ice
1 1/2 oz vodka
1/2 oz lime juice
Shake and pour over ice in a copper mug
Fill 'em up with ginger beer
Garnish with a lime

Can't miss! - Originated in Los Angeles in the early 1940s by a group of three individuals who were promoting their products: vodka (John Martin), ginger beer (Jack Morgan), and copper mugs (Sophie Berenzinski)

Strawberry Margarita

In a blender add
3 big strawberries
Jigger (1 1/2 oz) of tequila
1/2 oz triple sec
1/2 oz fresh lime juice
2 oz sweet and sour
Scoop of ice and blend that mother up
Garnish with slices of strawberry and lime

Shelter in place Wednesday! - This is a very popular and flavorful
variation of the Margarita. Easy to shelter in place with one of these

TEQUILA SUNRISE
In a tall glass
1/4 oz grenadine
Fill glass with ice
1 1/2 oz tequila
2 oz orange juice
Top off with soda water or 7-up
Float a splash of crème de cassis
Garnish with a lime wheel and cherry

The origins of the sunrise vary from Arizona in the 1930s or '40s to Cancun and Acapulco in the 1950s to Sausalito in the 1970s. Regardless the origin, this is a keeper in any cocktail guide

SUNSET BY MAUNALUA BAY
Fill a Collins glass with ice
2 oz light rum
1 oz orange juice
1 oz pineapple juice
Slowly pour in 1/2 oz grenadine

Maunalua was one of the first settlements in Hawaii around the 12th century. This is a fitting and refreshing Hawaiian drink as tribute to Maunalua Bay

A FANCY WHISKEY
Fill a cocktail shaker with ice
2 oz whiskey
1 dash Angostura bitters
1/2 oz triple sec
1/2 teaspoon super fine sugar
Shake until well chilled
Strain into a martini glass
Garnish with an orange or lemon twist

This is a variation of the Old Fashioned, but it's a vintage cocktail in its own right

AMERICANO
Fill a glass with ice
3/4 oz Campari
3/4 oz sweet vermouth
Fill with club soda
Garnish with an orange slice

This one belongs in the Hall of Fame (the cocktail does too) - A pure
aperitivo cocktail traced back to Milan in the late 1880s (Hint: for you
non baseball fans, that's Pete Rose's jersey in the background)

APEROL PALOMA COCKTAIL
Fill a cocktail shaker with ice
2 oz white tequila
1/2 oz Aperol
1 1/2 oz grapefruit juice
1 oz triple sec
1/2 oz simple syrup
Shake until well chilled
Strain into an ice-filled glass
Garnish with a slice of lime, lemon, or orange

Locked down, but not out! - The Paloma originated in Tequila, Mexico
and Aperol originated in Padua, Italy. Sometimes you can't decide what
cocktail you want. This gives you two drinks in one!

Cocktails Listed by Alcohol

Brandy Cocktails

- Brandy Alexander
- Cafe Amore
- Liberty Cocktail
- Pan-American Clipper
- Sidecar
- Stinger

Gin Cocktails

- Beauty Spot
- Berry Bramble
- Cobbler
- Eagle's Dream
- Espresso Martini
- French 75
- Gimlet
- Gin Fizz
- Gin Rickey
- Gin Rossa
- Japanese Gin and Tonic
- Lone Tree Cooler
- Maiden's Blush
- Martini Up, dry, with two olives
- Monte Carlo Imperial
- Negroni

Gin Cocktails, Continued

- Opal Cocktail
- Ramos Fizz
- Singapore Sling
- Stork Club
- Strawberry Dawn
- White Lady

Rum Cocktails

- Black Diamond Swizzle
- Blue Hawaiian
- Boston Cooler
- Bushwhacker
- Caribbean Cruise
- Daiquiri
- Dark and Stormy
- Dawn's Havana
- French Colada
- Pink Paradise
- Rum Relaxer
- Strawberry Daiquiri (Frozen)
- Sunset by Maunalua Bay
- ¡Venezuela Libre!

Scotch Cocktails

- Bonny Doon
- Hole in One
- Rob Roy

Tequila Cocktails

- Aperol Paloma Cocktail
- Jose and OJ
- Li hing Margarita
- Marble Queen
- Margarita Classica
- Margarita (Joe-Garita)
- Peach Margarita
- Pineapple/Mango Margarita (Frozen)
- Strawberry Margarita
- Tequila Sunrise

Virgin Drinks

- Shirley Temple
- Virgin Colada

Vodka Cocktails

- Blue Lagoon
- Chambord Lemonade
- Cape Cod
- Cosmopolitan
- Dave and Mike's Midori Illusion
- Deep Blue Sea Martini
- Espresso Martini
- Gangster Martini
- Loneliness
- Mango Sunset
- Martini up, dry, with two olives

Vodka Cocktails, Continued

- Midori Illusion
- Moscow Mule
- Naked Pretzel
- Pink Lemonade
- Rhubarb Pie
- Tropical Breeze
- Vodka Tonic
- Zipper

Whiskey Cocktails

- A Fancy Whiskey
- Cinnamon Maple Bourbon Sour
- Manhattan
- Old Fashioned
- Romeo and Julip
- Sage Brown Derby
- Sazerac
- Stiletto Manhattan
- Western Sour
- Whiskey Daisy
- Whiskey Smash
- Whiskey Sour
- Whiskey Squirt

LIQUEUR AND OTHER COCKTAILS

- Americano
- Blue Carnation
- Bocce Ball
- Campari Mint Spritz
- Cuban Almond
- Dolce Vita
- Dublin Iced Coffee
- Golden Cadillac
- Grasshopper
- Italian Spritz
- Italian Wine and Sambuca
- Kir Royal
- Raspberry, Limoncello and Prosecco cooler
- Wallis cocktail

REFERENCES

Craddock, Harry (2015). The Savoy Cocktail Book. Girard & Stewart

Difford, Simon (2001). Difford's Guide for Discerning Drinkers. www.diffordsguide.com

Giglio, Anthony (2008). Mr. Boston: Official Bartender's Guide. 67th edition with over 1500 drink recipes. John Wiley & Sons

Saucier, Ted (2011). Ted Saucier's Bottoms Up (With Illustrations by Twelve of America's Most Distinguished Artists). Martino Fine Books

Straub, Jacques (1914). Drinks. CreateSpace Independent Publishing Platform

Thomas, Jerry (2008). Jerry Thomas' Bartenders Guide: How to Mix Drinks 1862 Reprint: A Bon Vivant's Companion. CreateSpace Independent Publishing Platform

Index

A

B

C

Index

Index

Index

Index

Index

Index

Whiskey Daisy, 34-35
Whiskey Smash, 29
Whiskey Sour, 72-73
Whiskey Squirt, 42
White Lady, 62

Z

Zipper, 44

AFTERWORD

Who knows when opportunity will knock - or what it will look like when it does? This book began as a passing idea during a strange and uncertain time in our lives, and somehow, it turned into this finished collection.

What started as a creative outlet became a journey of experimentation, stories, and flavors. Along the way, we discovered that a cocktail is never just a drink - it's a moment, a memory, a conversation starter, or a connection.

If this book found its way into your hands, maybe it knocked on your door too. And if it made you smile, stirred a little curiosity, or inspired you to try something new, then we've succeeded.

To all the unexpected moments that push us forward - cheers!

And most of all, thank you for reading.

If you've enjoyed this book, please leave a review on Amazon. We read every review and they help new readers discover this book.

Acknowledgments

A big thank you to our wives, Donna Mastren and Dawn Dunbar, for their patience, encouragement, and participation throughout the lockdown.

Thank you to Kathi Lundstrom for her cooperation and enthusiasm in proofreading and editing.

Thank you to Julie Bawden-Davis for her availability and willingness to answer questions and for providing a path on how to get from picture-book to published book. (rosesareredpublishing.com)

Thank you to Lisa Brink whose extraordinary cover art really brought this book to life. (www.theBrinkCreative.com)

Thank you to all the people who encouraged us the write the book after seeing the photo book and trying some of our cocktails.

About the Authors

Dave Mastren grew up in the Lakewood and Long Beach area of Southern California, where he honed his bartending skills at beloved local spots including Fiddler's Three Bar and Galley, Adolph's at the Queensway Hilton, and McKenna's Creek. His journey eventually led him to Coeur d'Alene, Idaho, where he became a partner at The Ground Round—now known as Nosworthy's Hall of Fame.

Upon returning to Southern California, Dave took on the role of General Manager at The Naples Rib Joint, where he met his wife, Donna. He later left the restaurant world to earn a degree in Business and Management, launching a successful 30-year career in Information Systems.

Now retired, Dave enjoys golfing, baking, and—of course—entertaining. Drawing on many years of hands-on experience and a lifelong love of hospitality, he brings creativity, warmth, and authenticity to every cocktail he shares.

Dave Dunbar was born and raised in La Crescenta, California. While attending Chico State University, he landed his first bartending job at the popular Mexican restaurant La Hacienda. With no experience and plenty of pressure, it was trial by fire—but Dave thrived behind the bar and quickly discovered a life-long passion for crafting cocktails.

After college, he returned to the Los Angeles area and honed his skills at a number of Pasadena hotspots, including The Barkley, The Flintridge Inn, Barney's, and Brookside Country Club. Though he eventually moved on from California—and from professional bartending—his love for mixing drinks never faded.

Today, Dave lives in Hawaii, where his home bar is a regular gathering place for friends and family. He's still experimenting, still perfecting, and always ready to shake up something unforgettable.

With decades of experience crafting cocktails for everyone from locals to out-of-town revelers, the Daves bring a storyteller's heart and a bartender's precision to each recipe in this book. Their passion for classic and contemporary cocktails shines through on every page, offering readers not just a drink, but an experience.

www.ingramcontent.com/pod-product-compliance
Lightning Source LLC
Chambersburg PA
CBHW040854120626
46551CB00001B/20

* 9 7 9 8 9 9 9 2 1 1 0 1 9 *